Isaac Asimov's

21st Century

Library of the
Universe

Near and Far

The Birth of
Our Universe

OAKWOOD ES MEDIA
330 OAK MANOR DR
GLEN BURNIE MD

BY ISAAC ASIMOV
WITH REVISIONS AND UPDATING BY RICHARD HANTULA

Gareth Stevens Publishing
A WORLD ALMANAC EDUCATION GROUP COMPANY

Please visit our web site at: **www.garethstevens.com**
For a free color catalog describing Gareth Stevens Publishing's list of high-quality
books and multimedia programs, call 1-800-542-2595 (USA) or 1-800-387-3178 (Canada).
Gareth Stevens Publishing's fax: (414) 332-3567.

Library of Congress Cataloging-in-Publication Data

Asimov, Isaac.
    The birth of our universe / by Isaac Asimov; with revisions and updating by Richard Hantula.
        p. cm. – (Isaac Asimov's 21st century library of the universe. Near and far)
    Includes bibliographical references and index.
    ISBN 0-8368-3964-1 (lib. bdg.)
        1. Cosmology–Juvenile literature. I. Hantula, Richard. II. Title.
    QB983.A84   2005
    523.1–dc22   2004058938

This edition first published in 2005 by
Gareth Stevens Publishing
A WRC Media Company
330 West Olive Street, Suite 100
Milwaukee, WI 53212 USA

Series editor: Mark J. Sachner
Cover design and layout adaptation: Melissa Valuch
Picture research: Kathy Keller
Additional picture research: Diane Laska-Swanke
Artwork commissioning: Kathy Keller and Laurie Shock
Production director: Jessica Morris

The editors at Gareth Stevens Publishing have selected science author Richard Hantula to bring
this classic series of young people's information books up to date. Richard Hantula has written
and edited books and articles on science and technology for more than two decades. He was
the senior U.S. editor for the *Macmillan Encyclopedia of Science*.

In addition to Hantula's contribution to this most recent edition, the editors would like to
acknowledge the participation of two noted science authors, Greg Walz-Chojnacki and
Francis Reddy, as contributors to earlier editions of this work.

Printed in the United States of America

1 2 3 4 5 6 7 8 9 09 08 07 06 05

Contents

We live in an enormously large place — the Universe. It's only natural that we would want to understand this place, so scientists and engineers have developed instruments and spacecraft that have told us far more about the Universe than we could possibly imagine.

We have seen planets up close, and spacecraft have even landed on some. We have learned about quasars and pulsars, supernovas and colliding galaxies, and black holes and dark matter. We have gathered amazing data about how the Universe may have come into being and how it may end. Nothing could be more astonishing.

But the greatest drama of all is to try to understand the Universe as a whole. We can only begin to grasp its vastness and to study all the miraculous objects we find!

The Birth of Our Universe

Ancient Beliefs

Long ago, humans could only wonder about the vastness of the Universe.

To ancient people, Earth seemed to be no more than a patch of flat ground that was not very big at all. The sky seemed to be a solid dome that came down to meet the ground all around, at places not far off. People in ancient times thought the Sun traveled across the sky to give Earth light and warmth. The sky was blue when the Sun was present but turned black when the Sun set. In the night sky, there were many, many specks of light – or stars. The Moon, which went through changes of shape every month, moved among the stars. A few stars were brighter than the others, and they also moved.

Above: Ancient Egyptians thought of the sky as the starry body of Nut, the goddess of the heavens.

Above: According to ancient Greek myths, the god Helios drove a chariot carrying the Sun across the sky.

Above: The stars of summer gleam like jewels on the dome of the night sky.

Star trails in a time-exposure photo of the night sky. From where we stand on Earth, the Sun, Moon, planets, and stars all seem to wheel across the sky. It's no wonder people once thought Earth was the center of the Universe.

Above: Nicolaus Copernicus – the Polish philosopher, doctor, and astronomer who showed that the planets circle the Sun.

The Sun Is the Center

The ancient Greeks thought Earth was a large sphere located at the center of the Universe. They believed the Moon circled Earth. Outside the Moon's orbit circled Mercury, Venus, the Sun, Mars, Jupiter, and Saturn. Outside the orbits of all these bodies were the sky and the stars.

While it was possible to describe the movements of celestial objects in the sky in a way that fit this picture, it was very difficult. In 1543 a Polish astronomer named Nicolaus Copernicus showed that it made more sense to think of the Sun as the center of the Universe, with the planets moving around it. Copernicus stated that since Earth is one of the planets, it also circles, or revolves around, the Sun.

In 1718 the English astronomer Edmond Halley discovered that the stars moved, too.

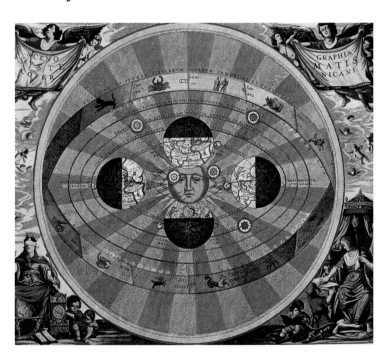

Left. The Copernican system, with the Sun at the center of the Universe.

Did the death of a star cause the birth of our star?

Our Solar System formed from a huge cloud of dust and gas nearly 5 billion years ago. Scientists say the cloud was rotating and gradually contracted into a disk, from which the Solar System developed. Did the cloud collapse simply as a result of its rotation and the gravitational pull of its parts on each other? One idea is that the supernova explosion of a nearby star nudged the cloud into collapse. That is not impossible, but supernovas are rare, and it is hard to imagine that enough supernovas occurred to cause all the dozens of planetary systems that have been observed.

Endless Galaxies

In 1785 the English astronomer William Herschel concluded that the stars formed a large collection shaped like a lens or thick disk. We call this collection the Milky Way Galaxy. This is our galaxy, and it is more than 100,000 light-years across. Each light-year is almost 6 trillion miles (9.5 trillion kilometers) long.

There are other galaxies as well. They look like cloudy patches in the sky. The closest large galaxy to our own is nearly 3 million light-years away. It is called the Andromeda Galaxy. Many other galaxies − large and small − are scattered throughout space. There may be be a hundred billion of them or more!

Left: Not only did William Herschel recognize our Milky Way Galaxy, he also discovered the planet Uranus and designed the best telescopes of his time.

Below: If we could view our Milky Way from a great distance, it would look much like the Andromeda Galaxy pictured here.

When the Andromeda Galaxy is viewed through a telescope, ragged dust clouds can be seen around its core. It lies close to 3 million light-years from Earth, and resembles our own spiral galaxy, the Milky Way. (The white streak across the sky is light reflected off an artificial satellite.)

Galaxies' Redshift

In 1842 the Austrian physicist Christian Doppler explained why anything noisy sounds more shrill when it comes toward you, and sounds deeper when it moves away from you. Light undergoes a similar change, or shift.

Every star sends out light waves. The light appears bluer if the star is coming toward us, and it seems redder if the star is moving away. In the 1920s, astronomers found that most galaxies show a "redshift." This means that they are moving away from our Galaxy. The more distant they are from us, the faster they are moving. The farthest galaxies are moving away from us at speeds of thousands of miles (km) a second or more!

Above: Austrian physicist Christian Doppler.

Below: Light from a star or galaxy spreads out into a rainbow of color. Dark lines appear where the light has been absorbed by the atoms of that star or galaxy. The lines are shifted toward ever redder light as the star or galaxy moves farther away.

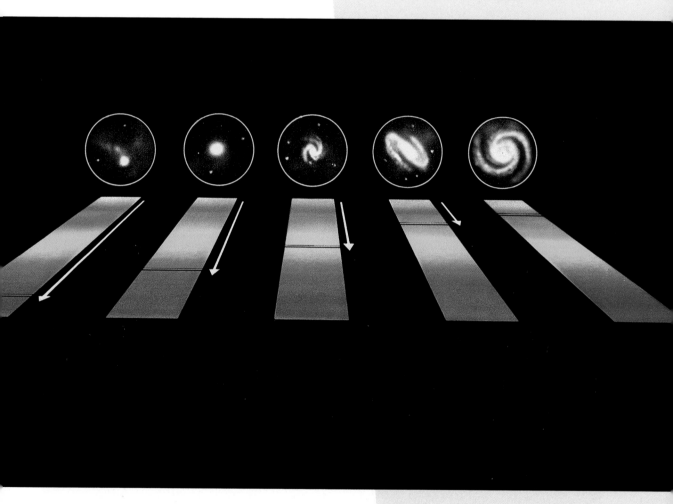

The Big Bang

Why are the galaxies moving away from us? The answer is that all galaxies are moving away from each other. The Universe is always expanding, and the space between galaxies is always increasing.

Imagine time going backward. The expansion of the Universe would go backward, too — the Universe would shrink. As we go farther and farther back in time, the galaxies move closer and closer together. If we go back far enough, all the galaxies will crunch together into a tiny space.

That was the way it was in the beginning. Everything must have exploded in a "Big Bang." The Universe is still expanding as a result of that Big Bang. If we measure how fast the Universe is expanding, and how long it must have taken to reach its present size, we know the Big Bang happened almost 14 billion years ago.

Above: A galaxy cluster. The glowing arcs in the picture are probably formed by light pulled off course by a tremendous, but unidentified, source of gravity.

Imagine that galaxies are like the raisins in raisin bread dough. The raisins start off fairly close together *(top)*. As the dough bakes, it expands and the raisins move away from each other *(bottom)*. As the Universe expands, the galaxies move away from each other, too.

13

The Big Bang's Echo

At the time just after the Big Bang when all the matter and energy of the Universe was still squeezed into a small space, it must have been very hot. The temperature probably registered in trillions of degrees. However, as the Universe expanded, temperatures cooled. Today, there are still hot spots, like the stars. But overall, the Universe has become much cooler over time. As the Universe cooled, the light waves of the vast flash of the Big Bang stretched and grew longer. Today, they are in the form of very long radio waves. In 1965, scientists detected these radio waves. They could hear the last faint whisper of the Big Bang of long ago.

The Big Bang's echo has been studied by special spacecraft - first the *Cosmic Background Explorer* (*COBE*), launched in 1989, and then the *Wilkinson Microwave Anisotropy Probe* (*WMAP*), launched in 2001. The results provided a picture of what the Universe was like not long after the Big Bang.

Above: *COBE*'s radio map of the Universe shows radiation from the Big Bang.

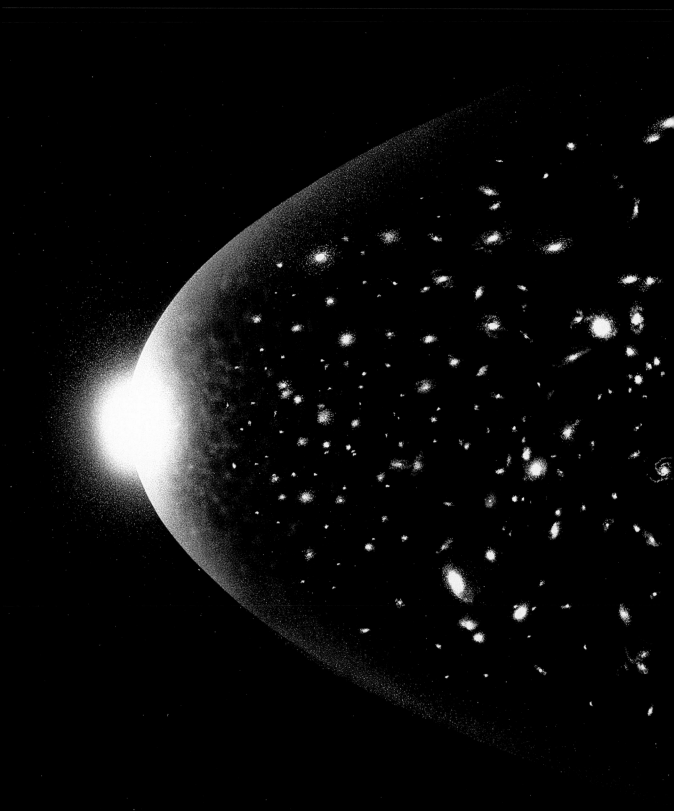

Our expanding Universe – the bright spot on the left represents the Big Bang. Farther to the right, subatomic particles form, then atoms of matter. Next, gas clumps together to form galaxies. Within those galaxies, gas further clumps together to form stars and planets.

The Universe in Infancy

Light travels at a speed of 186,000 miles (300,000 km) a second. If a star is 10 light-years from us, its light takes 10 years to reach us. Since the Andromeda Galaxy is close to 3 million light-years from us, its light takes nearly 3 million years to reach us. The farther out in space we look, the farther back in time we see!

Among the most distant objects that have been observed are those known as quasars. These give off enormous amounts of energy and are located at the centers of extremely remote galaxies. Light from the farthest known quasars takes more than 12 billion years to reach us. Since the Big Bang happened nearly 14 billion years ago, we see quasars as they looked when the Universe was quite young.

Also extremely distant are some objects that reveal their existence through the sudden release of huge amounts of the kind of radiation known as gamma rays. Scientists think that some of these "gamma-ray bursts" may occur when a certain type of immense star explodes in a supernova and collapses into a black hole.

Right: How far is far? Light from our Sun (*upper right*) takes just 8 minutes to reach Earth (*lower left of Sun*). Light from the triple-star system Alpha Centauri (*the bluish speck shown below Earth*) takes about 4.2 years to reach us. Light we see from the Andromeda Galaxy (*the large spiral galaxy at lower middle*) left that galaxy nearly 3 million years ago. Light from the farthest known quasars (*upper left*) set out more than 12 billion years ago.

Mapping the Universe

The Universe is not smooth but lumpy. Astronomers have discovered that galaxies seem to be usually located in "bubbles" surrounding regions of almost empty space called voids. This bubble-like structure probably developed from a slight lumpiness, or variation in density, that existed already soon after the Big Bang. This early lumpiness can be seen in maps made by scientists using data from the *COBE* and *WMAP* spacecraft.

Above: In a project known as the Sloan Digital Sky Survey, astronomers found the distances to galaxies (*right*) and then plotted a map (*left*) in which each galaxy is represented by a single point. The map is 2 billion light-years deep.

Why is the Universe like soap bubbles?

Throughout the Universe, galaxies seem arranged in lines and even curves. If we could look at the Universe from a great distance and see it all at once, we would think it looked like soap bubbles of all sizes. The bubbles enclose large spaces called voids in which there seems to be relatively little matter. Galaxies would be like the soap film making up the bubbles. The bubbles themselves would be more or less empty.

Below: After the Big Bang, temperature variations developed (*1*). Gravity caused matter to condense into clouds (*2*) and then into stars (*3*) and chains of galaxies (*4*), resulting in the billions and billions of stars and galaxies of today (*5*).

Right: Temperature variations in the Universe soon after the Big Bang, as detected by the WMAP spacecraft.

19

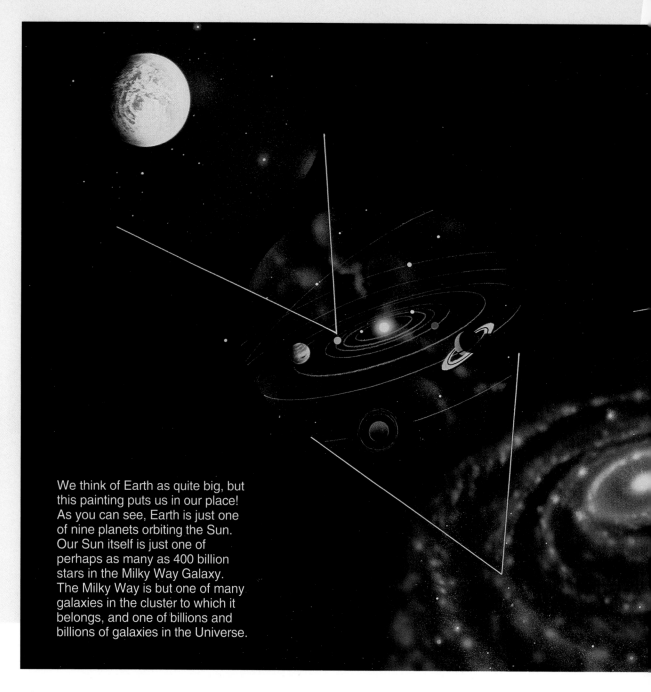

We think of Earth as quite big, but this painting puts us in our place! As you can see, Earth is just one of nine planets orbiting the Sun. Our Sun itself is just one of perhaps as many as 400 billion stars in the Milky Way Galaxy. The Milky Way is but one of many galaxies in the cluster to which it belongs, and one of billions and billions of galaxies in the Universe.

Our Vast Universe

The known planets orbit the Sun in a region of space that is only about 9 billion miles (15 billion km) across. That's less than one five-hundredth of a light-year. The nearest star after our Sun is 4.2 light-years away. That's thousands of times as far away as the farthest planet in our Solar System. The farthest stars in our Galaxy are about 100,000 light-years away. The Andromeda

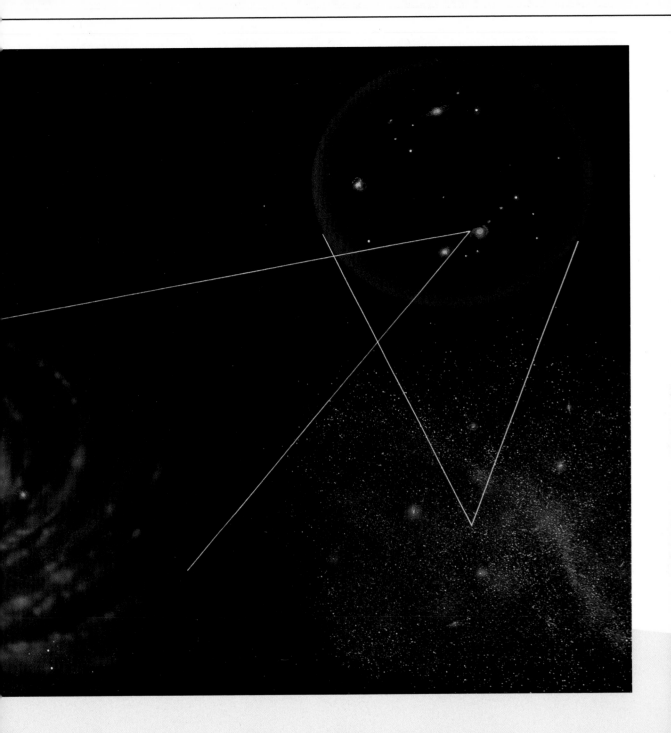

Galaxy is close to 3 million light-years away, but it's our next-door neighbor! The farthest known quasars are more than 12 billion light-years away. In all the Universe, there may be 100 billion galaxies or more. And each galaxy contains billions of stars. Some galaxies have more stars than our Milky Way. Imagine how small our own Earth is in comparison!

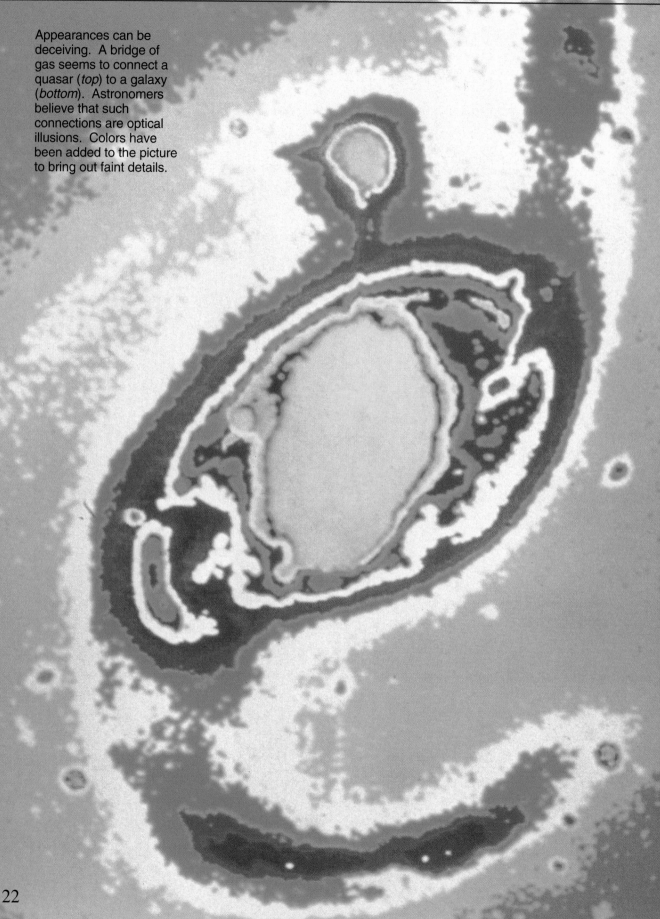

Appearances can be deceiving. A bridge of gas seems to connect a quasar (*top*) to a galaxy (*bottom*). Astronomers believe that such connections are optical illusions. Colors have been added to the picture to bring out faint details.

Quasars – From a Time Before Our Sun

In the 1950s, astronomers discovered certain objects that send out strong radio waves and that, when observed through a telescope, look like stars. These objects were given the name "quasi-stellar radio sources," or "quasars" for short. They were found to have the largest redshifts known. This indicated that they are located an incredible distance away and release enormous amounts of energy. Other extremely distant star-like objects that give off huge amounts of energy, although not necessarily radio waves, also came to be called quasars.

Scientists think quasars are objects at the centers of galaxies. The quasars that have been discovered so far are from 800 million to more than 12 billion light-years away. When we look at the oldest of them, we are looking back into a time before our Sun was born!

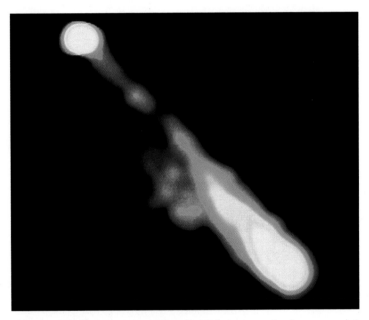

Above: Radio telescopes created this image of a huge gas jet erupting from a quasar called 3C 273. The jet is a million light-years long!

Some stars change in size!

Some stars change in brightness. Certain types of such "variable stars" pulsate, or grow larger and smaller, in a regular rhythm. The larger and brighter these stars are, the more slowly they pulse. Therefore, scientists can tell how bright they are from how quickly or how slowly they pulse. Scientists can also tell how far away the stars are from how bright they are. Scientists study pulsating stars in nearby galaxies to find out how far away the galaxies are.

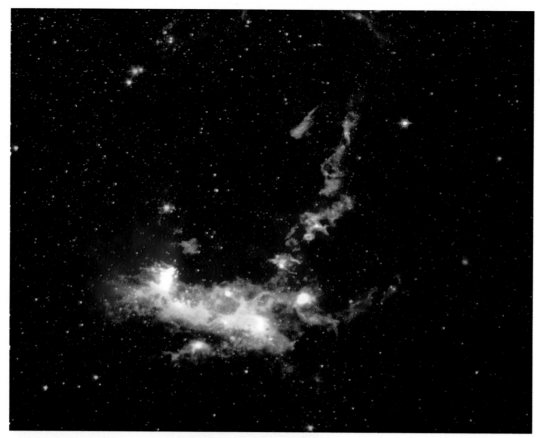

Above: The nebula called Henize 206. This cloud of gas and dust is a "stellar nursery." It contains many young stars, whose formation was assisted by the force of a mighty supernova explosion millions of years ago. *Below*: When Galaxy M82 nearly collided with a neighboring galaxy, it set off explosive bursts of star formation and shot off gas plumes thousands of light-years into space. Astronomers call M82 a "starburst galaxy."

A Supernova Beginning

Stars stay hot because of nuclear reactions in their centers. In the case of stars that are about the size of the Sun or larger, as the star center grows hotter, the star expands. But eventually, the star explodes and collapses.

When a very large star explodes, it becomes a supernova. Supernovas spread their material through space. In the Big Bang, only the simplest atoms — such as hydrogen and helium — were formed. But supernovas spread more complex atoms outward.

Our Solar System formed from a cloud that contained some of these more complex atoms. Many of the atoms of Earth — and also in ourselves — were formed in stars that exploded as supernovas long ago.

Above: Galaxy NGC 5128 before *(left)* and after *(right)* it had a supernova *(arrow)*.

A crab in the sky!

In 1054 a supernova only about 6,500 light-years away appeared in the sky. It was brighter than the planet Venus. A year or so later, it faded away. What is left of it can still be seen as a small, cloudy patch in the exact place where the supernova was. It is actually a cloud of debris left by the explosion. Because of its shape, it is called the Crab Nebula. It has been expanding for almost a thousand years since the explosion. In the Crab Nebula's center is a tiny neutron star. This is all that is left of the original giant star that exploded.

Big Rip or Big Crunch?

When an extremely massive star explodes in a supernova, what is left of it can collapse to form a black hole — an object whose gravity is so strong that everything falls in but nothing comes out.

Many scientists think that the expansion of the Universe is caused by a mysterious "dark energy" that works against the force of gravity. Scientists do not know what will happen in the future. Perhaps the Universe will keep on expanding forever. Or perhaps dark energy will cause the expansion to speed up to such an extent that at some point all matter in the Universe will suddenly fly apart in a "Big Rip." Or perhaps dark energy will weaken, allowing gravity to slow the Universe's expansion and maybe even stop it. The Universe might then fall back together into an enormous black hole.

Perhaps this "Big Crunch" might be followed by the formation of a new Universe in a new Big Bang. It might even be that there was a Big Crunch, or even many Big Crunches, before the Big Bang that formed our Universe. No one knows.

Opposite: According to one theory, someday in the very distant future the Universe may stop expanding and begin contracting. Then everything in the cosmos would fall into an enormous black hole (*top of painting*). Afterward, perhaps there would be another Big Bang!

Mini-stars with mega-mass

When a star explodes and collapses, it becomes incredibly smaller than you might ever expect. It's like breaking apart a Ping-Pong ball and then packing the pieces back together in a small, tight pile. Some stars collapse into white dwarf stars. White dwarfs can be smaller than Earth, but they can hold the same amount of matter as the Sun! Still smaller stars, called neutron stars, may be formed when large stars collapse. Neutron stars can contain as much mass as our Sun, but they might be only a few miles (km) in diameter!

Fact File: Our Universe – The Enormity of It All!

We know the Universe is a big place. But just how big is it? Imagine that we could make the Sun the size of a soccer ball. Then let's shrink the entire known Universe even further, so we could put the Solar System in a cup. And finally, let's shrink the Universe down so that our Galaxy, the Milky Way, would be no wider than this book!

Even after reducing the Universe this much, we might be surprised at how far apart everything in the cosmos still seems. Use the illustrations (above and opposite) and the information (opposite) to get an idea of how big and how far away everything in the Universe is. As big as we think Earth is, it is only a tiny speck in our vast Universe!

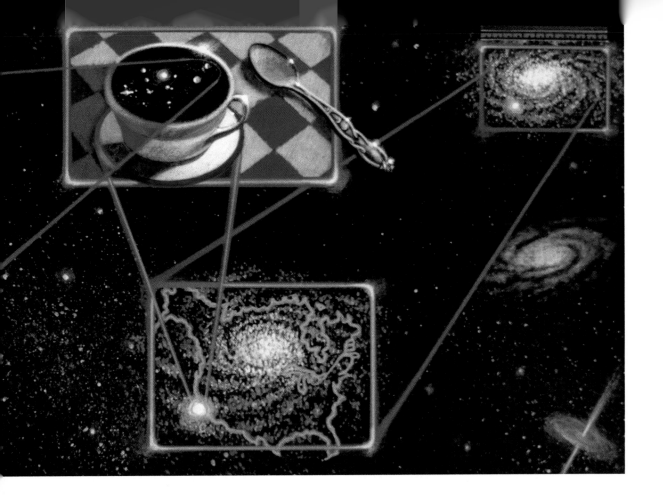

The Sun as a Soccer Ball

• What if the Sun were...a soccer ball about 8 3/4 inches (22 centimeters) wide?

• Then Earth would be...a pebble less than 1/10 inch (1/4 cm) wide, and about 78 3/4 feet (24 meters) from our soccer-ball Sun.

• And Jupiter (our Solar System's biggest planet) would be...a bit bigger than a small ball bearing that is 7/8 inch (2.2 cm) wide.

• And Pluto (our Solar System's tiniest known planet) could be...a pebble smaller even than Earth, about 1/2 mile (0.8 km) from our soccer-ball Sun.

• And Proxima Centauri (the nearest star in our Galaxy, besides our Sun) would be...almost 4 miles (6.4 km) from the soccer-ball Sun at the center of our Solar System.

The Milky Way as a Book

• And what if the Milky Way (our Galaxy) was... a book about 1 foot (30 cm) wide?

• Then the Andromeda Galaxy (the galaxy "next door") would be...about 29 feet (9 m) away from the Milky Way.

• And the farthest-known quasars would be...about 23 miles (37 km) away from the Milky Way!

The Solar System in a Cup

• And what if our Solar System (out to the orbit of Pluto) were...small enough to fit in a cup?

• Then the Milky Way (our Galaxy) would be... as wide as North America — about 3,000 miles (4,800 km) across!

More Books about Our Universe

Big Bang: The Birth of our Universe. Paul Parsons (Dorling Kindersley)

The Big Bang: What It Is, Where It Came From and Why It Works. Karen C. Fox (Wiley)

Exploring the Universe. Claude Lafleur (World Almanac Library)

The Extravagant Universe : Exploding Stars, Dark Energy, and the Accelerating Cosmos. Robert P. Kirshner (Princeton)

Power of Ten: A Flipbook. Charles Eames and Ray Eames (W. H. Freeman)

Smithsonian Intimate Guide to the Cosmos. Dana Berry (Smithsonian)

DVDs

The Creation of the Universe. (Paramount Home Video)

The Expanding Universe. (Image Entertainment)

Stargaze II - Visions of the Universe (Wea)

Web Sites

The Internet is a good place to get more information about our Universe. The web sites listed here can help you learn about the most recent discoveries, as well as those made in the past.

NASA, StarChild. starchild.gsfc.nasa.gov/docs/StarChild/StarChild.html

NASA, Wilkinson Microwave Anisotropy Probe. map.gsfc.nasa.gov/

PBS, Nova Online, Runaway Universe. www.pbs.org/wgbh/nova/universe/index.html

Windows to the Universe. www.windows.ucar.edu/tour/link=/the_universe/the_universe.html

Places to Visit

Here are some museums and centers where you can learn about our Universe.

Adler Planetarium and Astronomy Museum
1300 S. Lake Shore Drive
Chicago, IL 60605-2403

American Museum of Natural History
Rose Center for Earth and Space
Central Park West at 79th Street
New York, NY 10024

Carter Observatory
40 Salamanca Rd
Kelburn
Wellington
New Zealand

Museum of Science, Boston
Science Park
Boston, MA 02114

National Air and Space Museum
Smithsonian Institution
6th and Independence Avenue SW
Washington, DC 20560

Scienceworks Museum
2 Booker Street
Spotswood
Melbourne, Victoria 3015
Australia

Glossary

astronomer: a person involved in the scientific study of the Universe and its various celestial bodies.

atoms: the smallest particles of elements that can exist. Atoms release nuclear energy when joined together or split apart.

Big Bang: a huge explosion that scientists think created our Universe about 13.7 billion years ago.

black hole: a tightly packed object with such powerful gravity that not even light can escape from it.

dark energy: a form of energy that scientists think works against the force of gravity and promotes the expansion of the Universe.

dark matter: a mysterious substance that seems to be the chief form of matter in the Universe. It does not give off light or other radiation, but can be detected through its gravitational effects.

galaxy: a large star system containing up to hundreds of billions of stars, along with gas and dust. Our Galaxy is known as the Milky Way.

gravity: the force that causes objects like Earth and the Moon to be drawn to one another.

jet: a stream of fast-moving gas or similar material coming from the vicinity of an object such as a star or a black hole.

light-year: the distance that light travels in one year - nearly 6 trillion miles (9.5 trillion km).

Milky Way: the name of our Galaxy.

nebula: a cloud of dust and gas in space. Some large nebulas, or nebulae, are the birthplaces of stars. Other nebulae are the debris of dying stars.

neutron star: a very small tightly packed star that may form when a large star collapses. Much of the mass of the large star remains in the neutron star.

orbit: the path that one celestial object follows as it circles, or revolves around, another.

quasar: an extremely distant object that seems to resemble a star and gives off huge amounts of energy. Quasars appear to be located at the centers of galaxies, and their activity seems to involve an enormous black hole.

radio waves: electromagnetic waves that can be detected by radio-receiving equipment.

redshift: the apparent reddening of light given off by an object moving away from us. The greater the redshift of light from a distant galaxy, the farther away the galaxy is located and the faster it is moving away from us.

rotation: the spinning of an object around a line, or axis, that runs through it.

sphere: a globelike body. The ancient Greeks thought Earth was a large sphere at the center of the Universe.

spiral galaxy: a type of galaxy that is rather flat and has spiral arms coming from its center. Our Milky Way is a spiral galaxy.

Sun: our star and the provider of the energy that makes life possible on Earth.

supernova: the explosion of a star during which the star may become a million or more times brighter.

Universe: everything that we know exists and believe may exist.

variable stars: stars whose brightness changes. Some variable stars change in brightness and size regularly. Others are unpredictable.

Index

Born in 1920, Isaac Asimov came to the United States as a young boy from his native Russia. As a young man, he was a student of biochemistry. In time, he became one of the most productive writers the world has ever known. His books cover a spectrum of topics, including science, history, language theory, fantasy, and science fiction. His brilliant imagination gained him the respect and admiration of adults and children alike. Sadly, Isaac Asimov died shortly after the publication of the first edition of *Isaac Asimov's Library of the Universe.*

The publishers wish to thank the following for permission to reproduce copyright material: front cover, 3, 15, 16-17, © Paternostro/Schaller 1988; 4, 8 (upper), 10, Courtesy of Julian Baum; 5 (upper), © Sally Bensusen 1988; 5 (lower), © Frank Zullo 1987; 6 (large), © Anglo-Australian Telescope Board, David Malin; 6 (inset), AIP Niels Bohr Library; 7, Mary Evans Picture Library; 8 (lower), © George East 1978; 9, 12, 22, 25 (both), National Optical Astronomy Observatories; 11, 20-21, © Brian Sullivan 1988; 13, © Julian Baum 1988; 14, NASA; 18, © Astrophysical Research Consortium (ARC) and the Sloan Digital Sky Survey (SDSS) Collaboration, http://www.sdss.org; 19 (all), NASA/WMAP Science Team; 23, Science Photo Library; 24 (upper), NASA/JPL-Caltech; 24 (lower), Mark Westmoquette (UCL), Jay Gallagher (University of Wisconsin-Madison), Linda Smith (UCL), WIYN/NSF, NASA/ESA; 26, © Mark Paternostro 1988; 28-29, © Larry Ortiz 1988.